HOT STOVE TRIVIA

Kidd Russell

iUniverse, Inc.
Bloomington

Hot Stove Trivia

iUniverse books may be ordered through booksellers or by contacting:

iUniverse
1663 Liberty Drive
Bloomington, IN 47403
www.iuniverse.com
1-800-Authors (1-800-288-4677)

ISBN: 978-1-4620-6787-9 (sc)
ISBN: 978-1-4620-6786-2 (e)

Library of Congress Control Number: 2011960855

Printed in the United States of America

iUniverse rev. date: 11/30/2011

About the Author

Kidd Russell comes from a gifted athletic family with a strong affection for baseball. He was a star athlete in his younger years and was offered tryouts with several major-league teams. However, due to family commitments and health issues, he was not able to pursue these dreams. He remains a huge fan, student, and historian of the game.

To Debbie—my wife,
the love of my life, and my best friend

Contents

INTRODUCTION

From the final out of the World Series to the sounds of pitchers and catchers in late February, the game of baseball makes us wait. But as we wait, the excitement and drama continue. What might have been, what could have been, and what's about to happen we can only speculate. And that's the fun of it. Baseball is now a year-round sport, and it's undoubtedly at the top when it comes to trivia in the world of sports. So while the bats are dormant, let's have some fun. Test your baseball knowledge with these off-season Hot Stove Trivia Teasers and see how you rate. Each quiz consists of ten questions. You can rate your performance in each based on your score:

0–2	still in the bush leagues
3–4	playing at the A level
5–6	playing at the AA level
7–8	advanced to the AAA level
9–10	made it to the bigs

HOME RUN DERBY

1. Who holds the record for most pinch-hit home runs?

2. Name the player with the most opening-day home runs.

3. Who holds the all-time home-run record for designated hitters?

4. Who has the most home runs after reaching the age of forty?

5. Which player holds the record for most home runs in one month—Roger Maris, Sammy Sosa, Babe Ruth, or Mel Ott?

6. Which player holds the record for most career inside-the-park home runs—Ty Cobb, Tommy Leach, or Sam Crawford?

7. Who has the most career home runs as a teenager?

8. Mickey Mantle and Eddie Murray are the switch hitters with the first and second most all-time homers (with 536 and 504, respectively). Who has the third highest total lifetime for switch hitters with 350?

9. What Hall-of-Famer holds the record for winning seven consecutive home-run titles—Babe Ruth, Willie Mays, Ralph Kiner, or Frank Robinson?

10. Which of the following is the only major-leaguer in history to have two postseason grand slams: Mickey Stanley, Reggie Jackson, Jim Thome, or Johnny Damon?

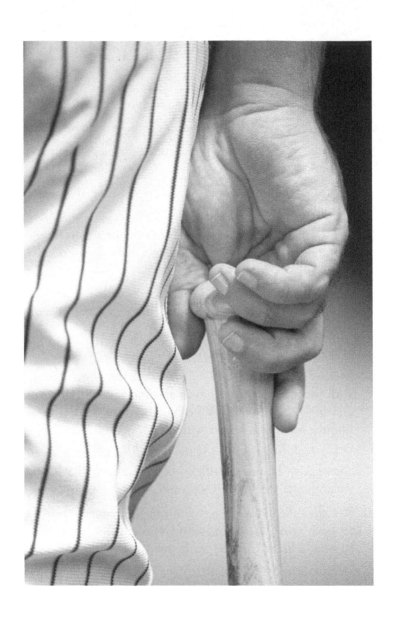

Answers

1. Matt Stairs with twenty-three

2. Frank Robinson with eight

3. Harold Baines with 225

4. Carlton Fisk with seventy-two

5. Sammy Sosa, who hit twenty home runs in June 1998

6. Sam Crawford with fifty-one

7. Tony Conigliaro with twenty-four

8. Chili Davis

9. Ralph Kiner (from 1946 through 1952) with the Pittsburgh Pirates

10. Jim Thome, with one in the 1998 American League Championship Series and another in the 1999 Division Series

Bet You Didn't Know

Name the slugger who hit more than sixty home runs in three different seasons and never won a batting title. Answer: Sammy Sosa, who hit sixty-six in 1998, sixty-four in 2001, and sixty-three in 1999.

PITCHERS' CORNER

1. Name the pitcher who holds the major-league record for career losses.

2. Twelve pitchers have hit a home run in the World Series. Name the two pitchers who have done it twice.

3. Who was the first pitcher to win the Cy Young Award in back-to-back seasons?

4. Name the pitcher who gave up Hank Aaron's 714th home run.

5. Name two of the three pitchers to win the Rolaids Relief Award in both the American League and the National League.

6. Who are the only two pitchers to lead their leagues in saves for four consecutive seasons?

7. Name two of the three major-league pitchers who have had both a twenty-win season and a forty-save season.

8. Who is the only major-league pitcher to win three World Series games for three different teams?

9. Who is the all-time leader of pitchers for home runs hit?

10. What three categories make up the Triple Crown of pitching?

Answers

1. Cy Young with 313
2. Bob Gibson and Dave McNally
3. Sandy Koufax in 1965 and 1966 with the LA Dodgers
4. Jack Billingham on opening day in 1974
5. Rollie Fingers, Lee Smith, and Randy Myers
6. Bruce Sutter (in 1979–1982) and Dan Quisenberry (in 1982–1985)
7. Dennis Eckersley, John Smoltz, and Derek Lowe
8. Curt Schilling (with the Phillies in 1993, the Diamondbacks in 2001, and the Red Sox in 2004)
9. Wes Ferrell with thirty-eight
10. Wins, strikeouts, and earned run average (ERA)

Dugout Dupe

Joe Sewell, an infielder in the 1920s and early 1930s, recorded only 114 strikeouts in 7,132 at bats, a ratio of 63 to 1.

NICKNAMES

Who are these guys? Match the players listed in the left column with their real names in the right column.

1. Sparkey Lyle   A. Johnnie

2. Bo Jackson   B. James

3. Bucky Dent   C. Richard

4. Catfish Hunter   D. Lawrence

5. Dizzy Dean   E. Vincent

6. Yogi Berra   F. John

7. Pee Wee Reese   G. Russell

8. Dusty Baker   H. Jay

9. Mickey Rivers   I. Albert

10. Goose Gossage   J. Harold

Answers

1. I
2. E
3. G
4. B
5. H
6. D
7. J
8. A
9. F
10. C

Fun Fact

Tom Seaver is the all-time leader in opening-day starts with sixteen: fourteen in the National League and two in the American League.

MVP AWARDS

1. Only two players have won multiple MVP awards and have not been elected to the Hall of Fame. Name both.

2. Ted Williams batted .406 in 1941. Who was the MVP that year?

3. Who is the only rookie to win the MVP award?

4. What major-league team has had the most MVP winners?

5. Only two shortstops have won two MVP awards. Name both.

6. Who was the first American League pitcher to win both the MVP and Cy Young awards in the same season?

7. What National League MVP was the second leading scorer during the 1951–1952 college basketball season?

8. Name the famous MVP whose brother finished second to Jesse Owens in the two-hundred-meter run during the 1936 Olympics.

9. Who is the only player to win the MVP award in both the American and National leagues?

10. Name the oldest player to win the MVP award.

Answers

1. Roger Maris and Dale Murphy

2. Joe DiMaggio (who led the Yankees to the Pennant)

3. Fred Lynn in 1975

4. The New York Yankees with twenty

5. Ernie Banks (in 1958 and 1959) and Cal Ripken (in 1983 and 1991)

6. Denny McLain in 1968

7. Dick Groat

8. Jackie Robinson (his brother Mack won the silver metal)

9. Frank Robinson (with Cincinnati in 1961 and Baltimore in 1966)

10. Barry Bonds in 2004

Hat Trick

Owen Wilson holds the all-time season record for triples with thirty-six in 1912. No one has come close ever since. Note that Wilson finished his career with 114 triples, not even in the top twenty all time.

FRANCHISE NICKNAMES

A brief quiz on team nicknames. Match each current major-league team with a former nickname.

1.	Red Sox	A. Broncos
2.	White Sox	B. Wolverines
3.	Tigers	C. Gorhams
4.	Yankees	D. Somersets
5.	Indians	E. Highlanders
6.	Cubs	F. Browns
7.	Dodgers	G. Invaders
8.	Cardinals	H. Quakers
9.	Phillies	I. Bridegrooms
10.	Giants	J. White Stockings

Answers

1. D (also known as the Pilgrims and Puritans)
2. G (also called the Pale Hose.)
3. B
4. E (also known as the original Baltimore Orioles)
5. A (also known as the Blues and Naps)
6. J (also known as the Colts and Orphans)
7. I (also known as the Atlantics and Robins)
8. F (also known as the Maroons and Perfectos)
9. H (also once called the Blue Jays)
10. C (also called the Green Stockings)

Out There

What former player labeled Don Zimmer the Gerbil during the 1980s? Answer: Bill "Spaceman" Lee.

GOPHER BALLS (PART 1)

Name the pitcher who served up the pitch for each of these famous home runs.

1. Bobby Thompson's "Shot Heard Around the World" in 1951

2. Bill Mazeroski's seventh-game walk-off home run in the 1960 World Series against the Yankees

3. Yankee Shortstop Bucky Dent's "Shocking Blast" in the 1978 playoff game against the Red Sox at Fenway Park

4. Blue Jay Outfielder Joe Carter's walk-off home run to win the 1993 World Series against the Phillies

5. Hank Aaron's 715th homer against the Dodgers in 1974

6. Roger Maris's 61st home run against the Red Sox in 1961

7. Mickey Mantle's "Gift Home Run" to pass Jimmy Foxx on the all-time list in 1968

8. Ted Williams's 521st home run in his last major-league at bat on September 28, 1960

9. Reggie Jackson's 1971 All-Star homer that cleared the roof at old Tiger Stadium

10. Gabby Hartnett's "Homer in the Gloamin'" walk-off home run against the Pirates in September 1938

Answers

1. Ralph Branca
2. Ralph Terry
3. Mike Torrez
4. Mitch Williams
5. Al Downing
6. Tracey Stallard
7. Denny McLain
8. Jack Fisher
9. Doc Ellis
10. Mace Brown

Round Trippers

Babe Ruth's sixty homers in 1927 were more than any team in the American League hit that year except his own Yankees.

GOPHER BALLS (PART 2)

Again, name the pitchers who gave up these big hits or famous home runs. All answers in this quiz are Hall-of-Fame pitchers.

1. Willie Mays's first major-league home run

2. Eddie Mathews's 500th home run

3. Hank Aaron's 600th home run

4. George Brett's famous Pine Tar homer

5. Kirk Gibson's 1988 World Series game-winning homer

6. Who holds the National League all-time record for giving up the most home runs?

7. Who has the most seasons (at seven) leading the major leagues in home runs allowed?

8. Who holds the season record for giving up the most home runs (fifty)?

9. Who allowed the most World Series homers?

10. Who served up Dusty Rhodes's 1954 World Series game one pinch-hit homer?

Answers

1. Warren Spahn
2. Juan Marichal
3. Gaylord Perry
4. Goose Gossage
5. Dennis Eckersly
6. Warren Spahn
7. Fergie Jenkins
8. Bert Blyleven
9. Catfish Hunter
10. Burleigh Grimes

Did You Know

Ted Williams hit a career total of 521 home runs and struck out only 709 times. In contrast, Reggie Jackson connected for 563 home runs and whiffed a record total of 2,597 times.

AROUND THE BASES

1. Name the first player to steal a hundred or more bases in a single season.

2. Who among these great players has the most steals of home: Rickey Henderson, Vince Coleman, Jacob Ellsbury, or Babe Ruth?

3. In 1946 when Johnny Pesky of the Red Sox held the ball for a split second, who was the slow-footed base runner who scored from first base to cop the World Series for the Cardinals?

4. Who is the only player to steal a hundred bases in back-to-back seasons?

5. Who is the only Triple Crown winner to have led the major leagues in steals?

6. Name the only three players to complete a season with forty steals and forty homers.

7. Who is the only member of the five-hundred-home-run club to steal over five hundred bases?

8. Who is the all-time major-league leader in caught-stealing attempts?

9. Name the last pitcher to steal home.

10. Name the all-time leader in steals of home.

Answers

1. Maury Wills

2. Babe Ruth

3. Enos Slaughter

4. Vince Coleman

5. Ty Cobb

6. Jose Canseco (1988, 42 HR/40 SB), Barry Bonds (1996, 42 HR/40 SB), and Alex Rodriguez (1998, 42 HR/46 SB)

7. Barry Bonds

8. Rickey Henderson with 335

9. Darren Dreifort of the LA Dodgers on June 12, 2001

10. Ty Cobb

Owners' Corner

Who did George Steinbrenner dupe as Mr. May following the 1981 World Series? Answer: Dave Winfield.

WHO SAID IT?

Name the player, manager, broadcaster, historian, or person connected with baseball who made the following famous statements.

1. "The other day they asked me about mandatory drug testing. I said I believed in drug testing a long time ago. All through the sixties I tested everything."

2. On Billy Martin: "I have no idea why I liked him so much. We never could figure it out. Me and Whitey Ford and Billy were all so different. That's why we got along so well."

3. "Reggie Jackson couldn't shine Willie Mays's shoes. He never hit .300, he's a butcher in the outfield, and he's got a big mouth. What does he make, $8,000 a week? I wouldn't pay him $8 a week. He's a bum."

4. "If I'd just tried for them dinky singles I could've batted around .600."

5. "Don't compare me to Babe Ruth. God gave me the opportunity and the ability to be here at the right time, at the right moment, just like he gave Babe Ruth when he was playing. I just hope I can keep doing what I've been doing—keep taking care of business."

6. "I can see how he [Sandy Koufax] won twenty-five games. What I don't understand is how he lost five."

7. "There's a little roller up along first, behind the bag! It gets through [Bill] Buckner! Here comes [Ray] Knight and the Mets win it!"

8. "Anybody who's ever had the privilege of seeing me play knows that I am the greatest pitcher in the world."

9. "[Barry] Bonds's records must remain part of baseball's history. His hits happened. Erase them and there will be discrepancies in baseball's bookkeeping about the records of the pitchers who gave them up. George Orwell said that in totalitarian societies, yesterday's weather could be changed by decree. Baseball, indeed America, is not like that. Besides, the people who care about the record book—serious fans—will know how to read it. That may be Bonds's biggest worry."

10. "Being with a woman all night never hurt no professional baseball player. It's staying up all night looking for a woman that does him in."

Answers

1. Bill Lee
2. Mickey Mantle
3. Leo Durocher
4. Babe Ruth
5. Sammy Sosa
6. Yogi Berra
7. Vin Scully
8. Dizzy Dean
9. George Will
10. Casey Stengle

Stenglese

Who was Casey Stengle referring to when he said, "I never play a big game without my man"? Answer: Yogi Berra.

RETIRED NUMBERS

1. Who was the very first player to have his number retired?

2. Name the only player to have his number retired by three different teams.

3. What number is retired by the most players?

4. What number is retired in all of baseball in honor of what major-league great?

5. True or false: Ty Cobb of the Tigers and Rogers Hornsby of the Cardinals do not have their numbers retired.

6. The only number seventeen was retired in honor of this great Major-league Hall-of-Famer.

7. Name the team that has the most retired numbers and how many it has.

8. What major-league team has officially retired the number 455?

9. Name the only two numbers to date between one and ten not to be retired by the New York Yankees.

10. Name the only two managers to have had their numbers retired by two different teams.

Answers

1. Lou Gehrig (number four, July 4, 1939)

2. Nolan Ryan (thirty-four by the Rangers and Astros and thirty by the Angels)

3. Twenty (retired in honor of nine different players)

4. Forty-two in honor of Jackie Robinson

5. True. Both Cobb and Hornsby played before the advent of uniform numbers but have uniforms retired in their honor by their respective clubs.

6. Dizzy Dean (on September 22, 1974)

7. The New York Yankees with sixteen

8. The Cleveland Indians (455 represents the number of consecutive sellouts at their home field from 1995 to 2001)

9. Two and six

10. Casey Stengel (thirty-seven by the Yankees and Mets) and Sparky Anderson (ten by the Reds and eleven by the Tigers)

Did You Know?

Johnny Bench is the only catcher to win a home-run title twice (1970 and 1972).

GRAB BAG 1

The last twenty questions are not related to any one specific category. Take your best swing at some of these teasers.

1. Can you name the two former major-leaguers who were Heisman Trophy winners?

2. Name the pitcher who recorded his 300th win and the batter who connected for his 3,000th hit on the same day.

3. Name the actor who played Babe Ruth in the original *Babe Ruth Story*.

4. Who are the only brothers to have won all four games of a World Series?

5. Derek Jeter collected his 3,000th career hit (all with the Yankees), a home run, on July 9, 2011. Who is the only other player to have hit a home run as number three thousand?

6. Besides Jeter, name the other three members of the three-thousand-hit club who wore a Yankees uniform sometime during their careers.

7. Can you name the infield players in Abbot and Costello's famous routine?

8. Name the only two Hall-of-Famers who were elected less than one year after their last games.

9. True or false: Willie Mays is the all-time leader in World Series home runs.

10. A ball batted past the pitcher hits the rubber mound and bounces into foul territory. What's the call?

46

Answers

1. Bo Jackson, who won it in 1885, and Vic Janowicz, who won it in 1950
2. Tom Seaver and Rod Carew on August 4, 1985
3. William Bendix
4. Dizzy and Paul Dean of the Cardinals in the 1934 World Series against the Tigers
5. Wade Boggs
6. Dave Winfield, Rickey Henderson, and Wade Boggs
7. Who, What, I Don't Know, and I Don't Care
8. Lou Gehrig in 1939 and Roberto Clemente in 1973
9. False. Mays had zero World Series home runs in seventy-one at bats.
10. Foul ball

Robbed

Did you know that Juan Marichal won twenty-five games or more in three different seasons (1963, 1966, and 1968) and never won the Cy Young Award?

GRAB BAG 2

1. Name the youngest player to hit a hundred career home runs.

2. Name the first five players elected to the Hall of Fame in its inaugural year, 1936.

3. Who holds the American League home-run record?

4. Name the Hall-of-Fame member who once played for the Harlem Globetrotters.

5. Name the Hall-of-Famer who lost the first World Series game.

6. Two players have won sixteen Golden Gloves. Name them.

7. True or false: Sandy Kofax was the youngest player elected to the Hall of Fame.

8. Name the only non–New York or former New York team to win a World Series in the 1950s.

9. Who is the only pitcher to hit two grand slams in the same game?

10. True or false: Carl Yastrzemski was the first designated hitter.

Answers

1. Tony Conigilaro
2. Ty Cobb, Walter Johnson, Christie Mathewson, Babe Ruth, and Honus Wagner
3. Roger Maris with sixty-one in 1961
4. Bob Gibson
5. Cy Young
6. Brooks Robinson (third base) and Jim Kaat (pitcher)
7. True. He was thirty-five when inducted in 1971.
8. The 1957 Milwaukee Braves
9. Tony Cloninger of the Braves
10. False. It was Ron Blomberg with the 1973 Yankees.

Brotherly Love

The Alou brothers—Felipe, Jesus, and Matty—played the outfield for the Giants on September 15, 1963 in a thirteen-to-five win over the Pirates. What Giant superstar sat on the bench that day? Answer: Willie Mays.